LESS

Other Books by Ian Gouge

Novels and Novellas

The Red Tie
17 Alma Road
Tilt
Once Significant Others
On Parliament Hill
A Pattern of Sorts
The Opposite of Remembering
At Maunston Quay
An Infinity of Mirrors
The Big Frog Theory
Losing Moby Dick and Other Stories

Short Stories

Dust, dancing
An Irregular Piece of Sky
Degrees of Separation
Secrets & Wisdom

Poetry

Bound
Grimsby Docks
Crash
not the Sonnets
Selected Poems: 1976-2022
The Homelessness of a Child
The Myths of Native Trees
First-time Visions of Earth from Space
After the Rehearsals
Punctuations from History
Human Archaeology
Collected Poems (1979-2016)

Non-Fiction

So, you think you're a Writer
Shrapnel from a Writing Life

IAN GOUGE

LESS

First published in paperback format by
Coverstory books, 2025

ISBN 978-1-0686701-6-9

Copyright © Ian Gouge 2025

The right of Ian Gouge to be identified as
the author of this work has been asserted
by him in accordance with the Copyright,
Designs and Patents Act 1988.

The cover image was designed by the
author using the Adobe suite of products
© Ian Gouge, 2025

All rights reserved.

No part of this publication may be
reproduced, circulated, stored in a system
from which it can be retrieved, or
transmitted in any form without the prior
permission of the publisher in writing.

www.iangouge.substack.com

www.iangouge.com

www.coverstorybooks.com

Contents

I

less 5
If we were Ancient Egyptians 6
Landfill 7
cyanide in the apple 8
collateral damage 9
comfort 10
Remembrance 11
Thirty mph 13
the carers 14
later 15
inside / out 16
when death comes knocking 17

II

belong 21
The Hit-count 22
hooked on ambition 24
a question of honesty 25
Sabbatical 27
off the main drag 28
First-term Crush 29
death of a gladiator 30
falling out of love 31
alibi 32

III

Interregnum 35
"Describe Keswick" 36
in Grenada (1986) 37
The Cottage Hospital 38
looking for signs on the motorway - 1 39
looking for signs on the motorway - 2 40
looking for signs on the motorway - 3 41
The New World 42
escape 43

IV

history lesson 47
baking bread in the bread-maker.................................49
They've taken down the signs for lunch 50
Life-lessons in Meccano 51
packing boxes for the removal van 52
Jackdaws 53
Red spider mites 54
Alternative Reality 55
Autumn Announced 56
The Schooner..57
Making Peace 58

V

oldest profession 61
Rue St. Denis..63
Foyle's 64
sinkhole 65
poems are sometimes like photographs 67
accident & emergency 68
short message service 69
countdown in the aftermath 70
betrayal 71
Words...72

❊

Acknowledgements..75

I

less

how did they scatter you
                         reverently
                         slowly

was a graceful arc described above the borders
by a hand knowing the flowers would be grateful
for the nitrogen
the base elements

and which way was the wind blowing

             the indignity of brushing ash
                   from well-manicured black

or were you mingled with many others in an unadorned trug

                   Chuck this lot out back, Pal,
                   and I'll put the kettle on.
                   Two sugars?

anonymity might have been the best fit
your life in microcosm

transient opportunities
                   (assuming there were some)
                                 thwarted by others
leaving you with nothing but memories of what might have been

like clinging to fragile black-and-white photos
and remembering that sunny Sunday
walking in the peace and quiet of the Memorial Gardens

If we were Ancient Egyptians

your decision might carry more import:
pine, rose, cherry
— or some heavyweight wood
long since made scarce by those
seeking luxurious passage
to the next life.

As it is
you baulk at the cost of the cremation
never mind the casket,
shy away from procession
and the empty words of a celebrant
who'd cram the night before
as if sitting an exam
whose outcome was in doubt.
Not that there would be much to say
— and to an audience of one at that.

"Cheap and cheerful"
doesn't cover it.

If there is guilt
(not simply for your frugality
but much more besides)
you accept the burden, find yourself
further disquieted by the realisation
that whatever you decide
could be a way-marker for your own falling
into Osiris' open arms.

Landfill

In the graveyard
trees a century old and more
have leeched all goodness from the soil
and taken to crushing coffins
with their muscular roots
in search of
life
        or so it seems.

In the far corner beneath the marque oak
two men decked out in black
scatter ashes nonchalantly.

If they could talk
what a waste the trees might say,
then return to their plundering and scavenging;
others' hopes and dreams distilled to chemicals,
the triumph of earth science
over those who need a name no longer.

cyanide in the apple

forget the snake
the consummate con-artist
that legendary slitherer
with its sibilant whisperings
and promises

it wasn't more you wanted
but less
or nothing at all

not difficult to work out

no need for a machine
the calculative whirring of discs
the smooth interlocking of cogs
but preferring the assertion of something personal
from which all else could be derived

they said the apple was red
gala?
red delicious?

empire might have been appropriate
not that it matters now

it's ironic you've left behind a test for us[1]
but a machine could never eat an apple
and maybe that's all the proof that's needed

---

[1] The Turing Test

collateral damage

Shejaiya, Gaza 15th December, 2023

fear pulled the trigger
veiled his dust-dry eyes
turned a white flag
to a symbol of defiance
the opening of a trap

fear pissed his pants
nothing more than that
no medical excuse
other than the inevitable
rush of adrenaline

fear made them cower
behind the shattered concrete
a burned-out bus
fear deafened them
to the ricochets of conscience

in the palace of politics
fear spills soundbites
from the guts of common sense
translated into a language
we pretend we understand

comfort

is a blue blanket
a square meal
water in the desert
a plaster on a cut
praise for effort
    for achievement
    for persistence

comfort
is something offered
    and freely given
    the outcome of an unselfish exchange

comfort
is something to be prized
    and celebrated
    and remembered
            fondly

eighty years ago
the Japanese army recruited sex slaves
    and comfort was taken
           stolen
    an unfair exchange
    involving the rape of the world

"Comfort women" were women and girls forced into sexual slavery by the Imperial Japanese Armed Forces in occupied countries and territories before and during World War II. - *Wikipedia*

Remembrance

Polished to a high gloss
his shoes pinch him as he walks,
not worn since twenty-eighteen
when they lost both Ron and Clive.

But today he is making an exception.

He looks at a field of knitted poppies,
elaborate shell-bursts of post-box covers.
When did ceremony cease to be reverent?
When did fashion take over?

More art installation than solemnity now.

Ron's 'Last Post' trumpeting was supreme
but the lad who took over that year
was flooded behind the ears
and didn't have a feel for it,

no scars to modulate his playing.

Perhaps that was when he walked away,
drew a line between remembering
and being seen to remember,
phoney demonstrations for media inches;

swore he'd do it his own way.

But now Marge has gone too
fallen on the beachhead of cancer
and loneliness has got the better of him
their house grave-quiet

like a trench before the shelling starts.

The shoes took him two days,
the shirt he ironed three times,
aired his old suit for a week
shaved twice in the space of an hour.

If you're going to do a thing…

That's what Clive used to say,
a phrase stolen from his dad
during a brief stint of leave
before a sniper got him in Normandy;

tells himself it was better that way.

He pauses half-way to the market square,
tries to resuscitate his ambushed feet,
pulls his regimental scarf a little tighter
then marches on.

Thirty mph

Blindsided by time's inaudible ticking,
when old age announces itself
— that pain in the hips
the need for new glasses
an extra wee in the night —
it is already too late.

You play records from your youth
and try to recapture an old self
(and what you've therefore already lost);
a sad kind of exorcism
with only one possible outcome.

Seeing their sudden benefit
you succumb to the idea of walking poles,
accept 'Nordic' into your vocabulary,
choose to regard a slight reduction in pace
as an opportunity to appreciate nature;

you take in the ambiance
of the farm shop café,
drive a fork into a slice of creamy carrot cake,
then return to your car (an automatic these days)
pop on the heated seats,
drive home well within the speed limit.

the carers

she
    sits stationary in her wheelchair
    leant to one side
    limbs folded
    like an abandoned attempt at origami

he
    bent forward
    leans in urgently to listen
    as if her words
    might be stolen away by the afternoon breeze

they
    have paused mid-walk
    perhaps as they might have dawdled
    many years ago
    arm-in-arm in the park
        she   pointing out a bird in the trees
        he   a rose blooming in the borders

but that is less than memory now
    she at his mercy
    and he
        in a way
            at hers

having heard what she said
    or understood what she wants
        not to be in the chair
        to be able to walk again
        to revisit the park of their youth
    he straightens as best he can
    and moves them on

later

when I'm dribbling down my front
ruining that expensive shirt you liked enough
to buy for nearly sixty pounds

or when my hands can't stop their shaking
and up-end the tea   Denby mug and all
shattering the handle into yesterday

or when I can't remember what day it is
when I last ate   or what I ate
nor my name   your name   our children

or when the Morris wallpaper in this room
reminds me of a place I've never been
or always went but never think I did

or when so much aches
I feel beaten-up   tenderised
into one purple bruise

when any or all of this comes to pass
I hope I remember
to say

sorry

inside / out

outside / a crow caws / grumpy and insistent / raspingly superior

    inside / waking early / I envy / its routine
    stitched into / the fabric of who / he is

outside / the sun rises / later by a minute / than yesterday

    inside / five o-clock / edges toward winter / and a timepiece
    grumbles / in time with / the crow outside

when death comes knocking

when death comes knocking
is it better to be prepared
to have an appointment
so you can be packed and ready
watch him as he saunters
self-assured up the garden path

or be taken by surprise
the sudden rap at the door
like an unexpected delivery
you assume is a scam

II

belong

beneath rain-heavy clouds caressing the horizon
I lift my pillowed head and wake to the window-flicker of sunrise
light cascading the hollow between the big trees
picking itself out in the puddles of last night's storm

early morning is the break between days
that instant when I find out whether I still belong

The Hit-count

She's put Trixie in the drawer
alongside blurred memories
and some neatly-folded remnants
of the person she used to be and
into which she can no longer fit.
When did she last try them on,
a final dance before the mirror of imaginary men?

It doesn't matter,
the Internet is her scrapbook.

In the supermarket chiller aisle
she watches mothers wanting more hands
to control trollies and children
as both slip through their clumsy fingers
finesse and subtlety long since abandoned.
Scanning for grated Cheddar
she wonders if they're really looking
for escape, or salvation, or love.
And as they walk away
slack-bottomed in too-loose jeans
she categorises shapes as if a pastime:
'child-bearing hips'
(the hips she had; the children she didn't).
Lifting Mozzarella by mistake and
dropping it carelessly into a basket
whose contents now define her,
she remembers what they used to say.

Her breasts were all adjectives.

But now they too succumb.
Too far gone for a comeback.
With a pang
she imagines Old Father Time

sniggering in the corner of the room
all the while she was humping,
moaning, licking lips at lenses,
going through the motions.

More tit, Love. More tit!

She avoids cameras now
much as she avoids that bottom drawer,
yet weakens just occasionally to check the hit-count
on the film of which she is most proud —
and where she imagines 'film' spoken with reverence
as if she were Streep or Taylor or Oscar-bound.

Nearly two million.
At least that's one thing
that won't be destroyed by time.

hooked on ambition

it was always a thin dream of course
sold as an adjunct
like a card in a packet of fags
an image of a footballer
      or a writer perhaps

      twenty silk-cut and a wordsworth please
      he's all i need for my collection

but it's another fucking larkin
and my album remains incomplete
just like the dream i suppose
something you cough your way towards
until the nicotine gets you

Cigarette cards were trading cards issued by tobacco manufacturers to stiffen cigarette packaging and advertise cigarette brands. Between 1875 and the 1940s, cigarette companies often included collectible cards with their packages of cigarettes. Cigarette card sets document popular culture from the turn of the century, often depicting the period's actresses, costumes, and sports, as well as offering insights into mainstream humour and cultural norms. - *Wikipedia*

a question of honesty

these he said *are the facts*
laid out just so   chronologically
because you know how much i like order

        as if regimentation makes things irrefutable
        precision suggesting sequence
        and not cold calculation

— i don't believe you

and why is that

— my truth is different

        and so he takes away his words
        deconstructs them to see how they measure up
        whether they resonate as they should

        holds them up to the light
        checks for flaws as he would a precious gem
        or perhaps a crack in a cheap ikea glass

        do they hold truth
        in the same way a glass should hold water

        then with a little shuffling
        he re-presents them
        flexing a little   adding nuance
        the benefit of looking at things
                                      slant

these are still the facts

— and this is still my truth

are you calling me a liar

and he wonders about the nature of lies
how words can be manipulated
how the same words in a different order
become something else   another story
facts stripped back to skeleton
thigh bone no longer connected to hip bone

or to any other bone come to that

encased in glass
                  cracked or otherwise
they could be relics
partly fractured
dug-up by a student archaeologist
on a field trip

these bones will become precious one day
the truth is always precious

— but that is not my truth and therefore it is a lie

    facts evaporate under a microscope
    if its lenses are looked through
    with the eye that's always closed

Sabbatical

Frances is taking a break from God.
He has become — unreliable.
It's the singing she misses most of all
even those new supercilious hymns;
and she wonders who has taken her regular spot,
front row just to the left of the nave.

Frances is taking a break from God.
Lee left high-and-dry, poor lad
(or Leigh, or whatever they call themselves now)
abandoned without a sex to cling to.

Frances is taking a break from God
dismayed by the killing in Ukraine
and the atrocities in Gaza
no matter the constitution or persuasion.

God is taking a break from Frances
concerned that she no longer understands.
He's gifting her some time to find herself
though He knows she'll blame Him for their falling-out.
And anyway, there's so much else to do.
Then God moves on, whistling a supercilious tune.

off the main drag

they've put up strip-lighting
on the outside of the big white house
at the corner of the road
presumably to emphasise the new patio
the swing-chair
the summer-only hot tub
but it makes the place look like an A1 adult store
not that the lights are red or pink
nothing so garish
but in the dusk the building glows
like a beacon or a spaceship

i've never met the people who live there
maybe they're aliens or have an imaginative social life

First-term Crush

Framed by toughened glass
you in silhouette above me on the stairs
at the apex of that charmless building
with its antiseptic corridors and cookie-cutter rooms
scarred with scuffs and memories.

What were you reading while you waited?
How long had you been standing there?

I recall a thick orange-spined Penguin.
Dickens perhaps. Or Bronte. Or *Middlemarch*.
I want to remember you cradling romance —
though if you carried such ambition to my room
I was too green and lily-livered to discover it.

Did I know the book and now forget?
Or did I never know?

I remember red hair; your height, tall for a girl;
a physique some might have said was statuesque.
My Echo has you studying Medicine at Boldrewood
and I regret, even now, how I never
became an object for your dissection.

What would you have found in my heart, I wonder —
and what would I?

death of a gladiator

we went on holiday to Rome
        in my dream

we took a bus to the Colosseum
        in my dream

we made love in the sun
        in my dream

in my dream
        we went on holiday to Rome
        took a bus to the Colosseum
        made love in the sun

i was eaten by a lion
        in my dream

in my dream
        you were the lion

falling out of love

you ask me to define it
as if I had etched upon the sky
clouds formed from something invisible

you ask me to justify myself
as if I had passed a law
removing all your privileges

you ask me to explain
how I could simply walk away
and not leave footprints in my wake

you ask me to come back
and bring words as wool for needles
so you can knit yourself back into my heart

alibi

when she finally parted her lips to let me in
I held her close with the longing of years
felt her hips hard against my body
tightened my grip to fuse our bones
to consume all of her
even that part she kept back for herself

later they called it murder
a strange term for something that was only ever love

III

Interregnum

Cigarettes clamped between their teeth,
they pull on bright nylon vests, dressed for teamwork.
Walking in practiced unison through the ruined heart of the city
and down to the mourning docks,
they recall once-hectic streets
and shopping for end-of-life care
when old age and death were matters of dull housekeeping.

Rusting three-dimensional hulks inform their future,
but national issues are slippery,
buried amongst twisted metal and soundbites,
slivers of routines and rituals pushed into voids
created by bombs and fire.
The unsavoury part of an unruly past
— nearing the end of its run —
is coming to a point where it might begin a second act.

Looking to the horizon they refresh an ancient faith,
long for sufficient rations to host a street party
at which to wave flags and point fingers for the suffering.
Nature peeks nervously through cracked dock-side cobbles,
market-stall fish scales glitter in puddles
sitting uncertainly in the landscape.
A cool breeze lifts off the quiet water.
The air tastes of low tide.

"Describe Keswick"

"Brooding.

Not Keswick itself of course
though in the razor-edged jags on garden-wall top-stones
there is an element of threat.

And slate grey everywhere
softened only marginally by white render
its brightness a partial concession
to something just out of reach.

And when they come
flocking by the coach-load to the B&Bs
are they also seeking the unobtainable
amidst the grey and white?"

"But 'brooding'?"

"When the low cloud swings in from the west
to envelop the top of Blencathra in an undeniable embrace
a cotton-wool of grey and white settles,
leaves the vaguest memory of what was once there
the only residual sharpness
found in razor-edged jags on garden-wall top-stones."

in Grenada (1986)

between Gouyave and Florida
there was a bend in the road so severe
you had to take it in first
slower than you could walk

tighter than ninety degrees
it fell away like a rollercoaster
that moment when you're plunged downward
your life accelerating away from you

decades of tropical storms
carved ruts into traps for tyres
like scalextric grooves from which the only escape
was to fly from a corner undone by ambition

you took that like a local they said

struggling with guilt
he assumed it was a compliment
no matter he was driving a hired four-by-four
had money in his pocket
white in his skin

The Cottage Hospital

after "The Cottage Hospital", by John Betjeman

Beyond municipal green, a maudlin wall
splits boisterous park from red-brick castle-tall

muddling town. Here under viridian trees
Sunday-roasting families still hope for breeze

as small uncorked children gallivant and try
to mimic the zig-zag of a mazy fly

as blindly it falls prey to a spider's weave.
No slow calypso mourning song sung to grieve

for such insignificance, no rescue call
made to squat and timid cottage hospital

where unanswered phones echo the parquet'd oak
while patients bereft of navigation soak

in sweat behind antiseptic pastel screens.
Matron knows that my fate too will go unseen,

faint rasping groans of the cemetery-bound
inconsequential. She dreams herself unwound,

there beneath full fruit trees as wasps and aphids
fly-on, serenaded by the life-filled kids.

looking for signs on the motorway - 1

signs

not the big blue ones overhead
with their highway gothic font
and ever-decreasing (or ever-increasing) numbers

nor those adorned with crude arrows
teasing at a nirvana which might be hiding
somewhere off to the left

but the signs you can't see
in the rumble of the tyres
in the chatter and then the silence

from the back seat
in the prompting from the sat-nav
or your voice second-guessing

everything

looking for signs on the motorway - 2

as i drive i allow my mind to wander
take advantage of an autopilot
brainwashed these forty years

>   once in a bristol city-centre street
>   i was hit by an old man's cortina
>   emerging slowly from a side road
>
>   *sixty years i've been driving
>   and never had an accident*
>
>   he was trying to blame me
>   and missed the confession
>   in his words

then the traffic slows
and i see the stationary snake ahead
and want to know how far into the distance it stretches

looking for signs on the motorway - 3

you drive too slowly   too cautiously

you leave it too late to move out
       or move in too soon

you complain about some git
being *right up my arse*
but refuse to give him the finger
when he finally speeds by

trapped in the passenger seat
i want you to pull over
for us to swap places
so that i can drive
       too fast   less cautiously
       my middle finger always ready
       for the dick who can't drive as well as me

The New World

captured on your smart-phone

    a mineral-streaked alcove
    horizontal bands of colour
    telling the story of the world

    a ruin of loose-stacked stones

    a bone-dry canal clogged with poison ivy

    and there a subtle line in the earth
    betraying the ghost of an ancient track

this was once sensitive terrain
where winds ruffled the canopy
its past   shadowed by ruins
cultures buried under cultures
skeletons hinting at a battleground of collisions

cluttered with artefacts
new towns fill with people making lives and families
and politicians
parade like Lears in pin-stripe suits
begging obedience   before blasting a road or
chain-sawing through a maze-hedge
    self-deluded architects of flimsy immensity

roughed-up by cautionary tales
weary experience tries to ally the old with the new
watches language fail to articulate a change in the rules
succumbs to an uneasy alliance fearing the status quo

escape

when the money ran out
sometimes he would sell toys for cash
a Hornby Pacific loco — with steam! —
traded for half-a-dozen sausages
a tin of carrots
Cadbury's Smash

  it was an odd exchange
  as if they had landed in a foreign world
  with a different currency
  where joy and innocence had been devalued
  their investments lasting no more than a week

    he was a refugee of sorts
    banished from his native shores
    forced to acquiesce to new rules
    imposed by those who should have known better

      and if there was a bunker
      in which he could settle
      undisturbed

        he did so
        locking the doors to his mind

          inventing new worlds to live in

IV

history lesson

you take a walk through the park
expecting to see rhododendrons busy
demonstrating their ability to infest
to encroach upon paths
leaning in as if for a quick chat
a natter over the fence
the blowsy cacophony of attention-seekers

but they are not there

a notice proclaims their culling as if a triumph
and lauds the desire for reacquaintance with a history
before the invaders came

in the void left behind
the un-mulched debris of earth now open to the sky
is matted by too persistent rain and
vulnerable to the punctuation of unfettered weeds

bored by neat verges and re-manicured lawns
you recall the chaos
assume trowel-carrying barrow-pushers
know what they're doing

I miss the colour you say
to no-one in particular
wonder if anyone will notice in your voice
how its regret will be never-ending

Soon the park will be as it once was
you're told
We'll reconnect with our past

and you wonder about your own past
how your journey across the years

has been marked by watching rhododendrons grow
and how a future bereft of them
might be like revisiting a history you're unable to remember

baking bread in the bread-maker

the flimsy booklet of recipes
now stained and dog-eared
prescribes weights and measures to the nearest
    gram   millilitre   teaspoon
knowing all the while that to stray
up or down   just a little
will not spoil the outcome

unless you overdo the salt perhaps

there can come a point where you have gone too far
    or not far enough
only later making the discovery
that you have created something unpalatable

which   in a way   is a little like life
    though we've no recipe book to guide us
    flimsy or otherwise

They've taken down the signs for lunch

'Remember that Lobster Bisque in Bruges?
Our steaks that melted on the tongue?'
— and the handwritten receipt we kept, now lost,
as if that could ever be enough.

Ghosts on a naked blackboard.
Traces of Chef's specials once chalked in florid script,
the enigma of ingredients
a code no longer on the menu to be broken.

Lured by amuse-bouches, we toyed with morsels
mistaking them for sustenance,
spices dancing more in imagination than on the tongue
a sprinkle of salt an inadequate stand-in.

Our options were infinite a lifetime ago
a mouth-watering cascade of things to try
until past their sell-by when one by one they vanished
rubbed out by an unseen hand.

Life-lessons in Meccano[2]

If they gifted you a silver spanner
as birthright —
        one end open   right-angled
        designed for awkward spaces and
        gaps too small for keen fingers
— that would help.

In plastic compartments
baseplates and connectors
        two-   four-   eight-holed
        triangles in snazzy yellow
        and wheels and bolts and nuts
        and those oh-so-silver washers.

I remember a tall crane
construction booklet-led
then inserting batteries   and watching
the hook rise and fall
until the string tangled and broke.

We fabricate our lives like Meccano
missing the invisible transition
        from toy to something else
        where taking apart and starting again
        shifts from anticipation of change
        to where doing so
                is suddenly impossible.

---

[2] "Meccano is a brand of model construction system created in 1898 by Frank Hornby in Liverpool, England. The system consists of reusable metal strips, plates, angle girders, wheels, axles and gears, and plastic parts that are connected using nuts and bolts. It enables the building of working models and mechanical devices." (Wikipedia)

packing boxes for the removal van

is like finding memories on a shelf
dusting them down for momentary reliving
before slipping them into a cardboard box
to be wed to the dark by extra-strong tape

presumably to be exhumed later

in the space on the box marked *contents*
with optimistic permanent-ink marker
you write MY LIFE in capital letters

Jackdaws

peeling from beneath the railway bridge
jackdaws scribe the air
like obsolete punctuation marks
slip the tyranny of girders
perch on barbed-wire fences
and hyphenate the landscape

Red spider mites

Lacking the order of ants, they chaos
across the patio in search of sap;

the Internet informs that's what they love.
Summer unfurls, suddenly baked and dry.

Grown hot, my daughter retreats to the house
the soles of her pale slippers dotted red.

Alternative Reality

Now there is a Government mandate / for every member of society / all adults born before a certain date / (when exactly? we're seeking clarity) / to be compulsorily arraigned / to star in Reality TV glitz / a programme chosen by algorithm / based on a non-binary attribute list: / like whether or not you go to the gym; / your base intelligence (or otherwise); / your adherence to the prevailing hymn / of beauty; ability to disguise / the shallowness of your ambition.

Not one exception.
No malingerers. We're all
non-entities now.

Autumn Announced

The door pulled open.
A sharp blast of cold air
the house breathes in.

The bird-feeder's water tray
first-frosting toward frozen;
the seed-stack almost emptied
in yesterday's frenzy
as if they knew what was coming

the chaffinches
the sparrows

as if they knew what was coming.
In yesterday's frenzy
the seed-stack almost emptied;
first-frosting toward frozen
the bird-feeder's water tray.

The house breathes in
a sharp blast of cold air;
the door pulled open;

autumn announced.

The Schooner

when through the fog the spectral ship appeared
silent before us on the running tide
torn sails spoke of the stormy seas she'd steered

on deck those ghostly pallid faces peered
as we fell mesmerised and open-eyed
when through the fog the spectral ship appeared

legend said this old schooner should be feared
and though such myths and legends often lied
torn sails spoke of the stormy seas she'd steered

as yellowed and gently swaying lamps neared
our shouts rippled out from the harbour-side
when through the fog the spectral ship appeared

on point the splintered figurehead now reared
her cannon-blasted features gaping wide
torn sails spoke of the stormy seas she'd steered

then rumour spread of how she had careered
through our scattered foes on the running tide
when through the fog the spectral ship appeared
torn sails spoke of the stormy seas she'd steered

Making Peace

Ingredients

- two cups of hope
- half a pint of water
- a sprinkling of salt
- a thousand grains of sugar (or one small sugar cube)
- yeast (preferably fresh)
- some stock (made from distilled patience and persistence)

Method

1. mix the hope and water
2. add the salt and sugar (the cube crushed if a cube is used)
3. stir
4. add the yeast and stir again
5. finally add the stock
6. mix well and leave to rise

— or to ferment
even though fermentation is an odd word
in the context of making peace

when ready
share liberally
throw parties in celebration

NOTE 1: THE MIXTURE IS OFTEN LEFT IN THE DARK, WHICH RESULTS IN THE INGREDIENTS FAILING TO BOND

NOTE 2: THE MIXTURE SHOULD BE KEPT IN THE LIGHT; CHECKED REGULARLY; COSSETED LIKE A SOURDOUGH STARTER

NOTE 3: THE PARTY WILL NOT BE FOR YOU BUT FOR YOUR DESCENDANTS — AND ONLY IF YOU HAVE BEEN DILIGENT IN PREPARING THE INGREDIENTS AND FOLLOWING THE METHOD

V

oldest profession

1

words are predictably unoriginal
lying on their backs and turning tricks
for a few sou (or some other redundant currency)
dropped into a chipped saucer
on a sideboard that has been better days

perhaps they are saving up for something
liberation perhaps
the opportunity to jack it all in
head off to where they can be fulfilled
and sunsets are real

2

the punters
having got their breath back
pulled their kecks up
pause at the end of the non-marital bed
avoid the mirror on the dresser

released into an unoriginal landscape
collar up they shuffle away
hoping to remain inconspicuous
hoping no-one will cotton-on
put two and two together

they only meant to try it once
just an experiment
the idea foist on them by an ex-friend
who told them the experience
would be liberating

it's the opposite of course
an addiction of the first order
compulsion emptying their wallet
what's left of their heart
the ink in their biros

Rue St. Denis

They parade semi-naked about the place
like mantlepiece garniture flashing its
art nouveau credentials: the cold ripple of
an onyx base; skin disguised as bronze; figures
lithe and elegant with serpentine movements
in the wrists, the arc of a thigh; the treasure
trove of nipples, pudenda worn to gleaming.
Fool's gold, the lure of glazed spelter.

Or if not semi-naked then seeming so.
Promise teases with a glimpse of what
awaits, tantalising anticipation
releasing the torture of the possible.
Untroubled by the lives they unravel, they
loiter, knowing how the gentle beckoning
of a finger points to something — your future
or perhaps even prescience of your past.

Foyle's

(Birmingham railway station & Charing Cross Road)

the shelves are riotously coloured
as if some bountiful god has descended
and with brushes of breathtaking bounty
dashed-off parallel vertical strokes
reimagining an ancient artistic movement

the heavy carpet absorbs sound
       the outside drone of the station announcer
       the rumbling of a nearby bus
       the throbbing of incessant traffic

it doesn't matter where you are
(cocooned like this you could be everywhere)
for in each brushstroke is another world
and inked in the atoms of these iridescent spines
the lives and worlds of others
landscapes so artfully rendered
you can almost smell
    almost see
    almost hear
        a different station announcer
        another rumbling bus
        the musical thrum of impossible traffic

sinkhole

impressed by some anonymous machine
a word is inked on a page

re-homed and the page left open for reading
the word becomes heavier than the world
eventually to shatter a coffee table's legs
under the weight of its meaning
turns the carpet to a sinkhole
disappears into the void
its absence making the news
and a flaky package where a trainee journalist
striving to strike the right degree of awe
intones *this is where the word was last seen*
as if it were some renegade escaped from an institution
with a dubious track record for security

which in a way is true

not just the institution
but the shed
        the page
                the sinkhole
into which falls not just the ink
but the meaning of the ink

what did the word say?
asks the journalist to an eye-witness
a man in a shabby coat which has seen better days

he shuffles on his feet
as his own words shuffle in his mouth
       or in his mind
plotting their own escape

I couldn't see it clearly

the reporter nods not knowingly
but those who do know
who've witnessed their own sinkholes
localised disappearances of words they once considered friends
simply turn their backs and walk away

they have come to terms with loss
or at least found a way to deal with it
a sigh   a shake of the head   a knowing glance
as if conspirators in a long-running battle
they know they cannot win

i think there might have been an 'i' says the eye-witness
keen to keep the camera focussed on himself

and so the journalist nods again
turns to the sinkholed viewers at home
attempts a reassuring tone in their signing off

poems are sometimes like photographs

sketching a life in fragments
occasional impressionistic pieces
you hope might one day coalesce
to form something coherent

this was me you want to say

and then
to examine each piece in turn
identifying a place   a person
your mother's third wedding-day
that uneventful holiday in Greece
the love of your life
       before the second love of your life
            (and so on)

but all too often you find the images blurred
their language letting you down
as if the autofocus was on the blink

either that
or you see the same thing depicted over and over
tourist shots of trees by a lakeside
a picture-postcard waterfall
the big hills still in the distance

was this me you end up asking

disappointed by your clumsiness with composition
your inability to sharpen edges or refine colours
you are wearied by the sameness of a life in monochrome

accident & emergency

like a surgeon
my finger hovers above the delete key
contemplating an incision
removal of a blemish   a cancerous growth
aiming then to stitch the wound
with other keystrokes knowing
the patient may not survive

should i leave such operations to consultants
close the laptop lid (lights out in the theatre!)
hang up my white coat
abandon the antiseptic corridor and walk away
hoping to one day find
a more suitable occupation
content not every one died

short message service

not delivered! in a small red font
the exclamation mark like a muffled shout
more observation than warning
   "you should be aware"...

where does it go   the undelivered message
despatched from the insecurity of a mobile phone
— insecurity arising from communication's weakness
not any existential threat —
and invisibly
            out

imagine it leaving the house through an open door
then down the path   traffic-dodging on the street
finding a open-armed mast
to propel it fibre-fast to its twin
                across another road
                      through another door
except

what if the other door is closed
its owner long since left
(a change of number perhaps)
or the gate is simply barred

does the message sit forlorn on the stoop
or scuttle away to electronic landfill
degrading according to some half-life
not toxic
      not anything

and how can you know

not delivered!   even in red   tells you nothing

countdown in the aftermath

in the corner of the room
a remorseless clock ticks
like the slow dripping in a drainpipe
long after the rain has ceased

without needing to be wound
it accompanies the sun
        the light
                the clouds that brought rain

and landmarks are mealtimes and sleeping
    and turning pages on poetry
    crafted by those whose
    manifestos I do not understand
    their gimmickry tapping to a different beat
    exposing the wasteland of my search

    and words that mine frustration
        boast of their power
            rejoice in my anguish
                tease me with the silence
                I know is coming

betrayal

what do they call it when a whisper echoes back louder than when sent out   when it's amplified by darkness as if invisible hands are cranking up the volume   a whisper which comes back as a softly-spoken question   then a statement   the expression of surprise   an exclamation a shout   for there must be word for those words   the ones that bounce around within the confines of our skull and then re-present themselves in oh so familiar garb pretending they're old and trustworthy friends when really they're something other entirely

Words

draw you in, collapsing spaces as
they fracture time, twist nothingness into walls
then make walls melt. You believe in their power
and what they might whisper, inspire, or unlock.

Acknowledgements

- "inside / out", "Life-lessons in Meccano", "Describe Keswick", "They've taken down the signs for lunch", "First-term crush", "The Cottage Hospital", "escape" and "Words" were all first published in the anthology *At the Edge of Fraying History*, Coverstory books, 2024
- "If we were Ancient Egyptians" was first published in *Ticking Clock Anthology*, January 2024
- "death of a gladiator" was first published in *The Aesthete*, September 2024
- "history lesson" was long-listed in the Bridport Poetry Prize, 2024
- "Interregnum" is based on 'Walking Tokyo' by Neil Shea from *National Geographic*, April 2019
- "The New World" is based on 'Battle for the American West' by Hannah Nordhaus from *National Geographic*, November 2018